# A book about birthdays

for_____

from_____

# Party Now, Age Later!

Created by
Jim Davis

Written by
Jim Kraft & Mark Acey

Illustrated by
Paws, Inc.

Andrews and McMeel
A Universal Press Syndicate Company
Kansas City

ISBN: 0-8362-0931-1

There's an art
to aging
disgracefully!

**Birthday Tip #54:
Never accept
a gift with
air holes!**

Somewhere out there is a cake with your age on it.

**H**ow about some cake with those candles?

A fool and his cake are soon parted.

# Birthday
## Party Tip #9:
## Get the negatives!

Overheard at a great party: "Water balloons at twelve o'clock!"

Overheard at a great party:
"I love the way this dip squishes between my toes."

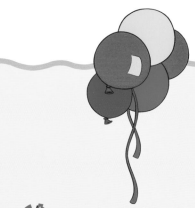

**O**verheard at a great party: "Who am I, and where did I get this chicken?"

Party till the
cows come home...
then party
with the cows!

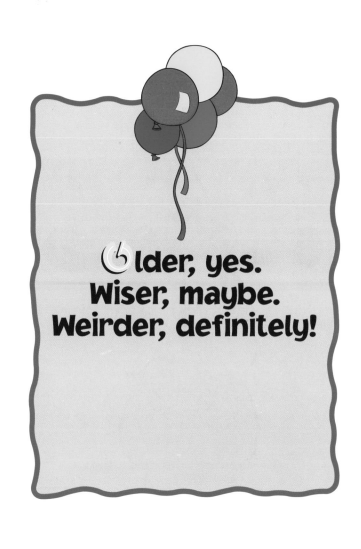

Older, yes.
Wiser, maybe.
Weirder, definitely!